T0099900

Walking *the* Tightrope

The Four Checkpoints of the Christian Profession

by

JAMES UGWUOGO

Power To Reign Ministries World-wide

WESTBOW
PRESS
A DIVISION OF THOMAS NELSON

Unless otherwise indicated, all Scripture references are taken from the New
International Version Translation of the Bible (c) 2011 by Zondervan

WestBow Press books may be ordered through booksellers or by contacting:

WestBow Press
A Division of Thomas Nelson
1663 Liberty Drive
Bloomington, IN 47403
www.westbowpress.com
1-(866) 928-1240

All internal image concepts were by the Author; image sketches were by Niyi.

ISBN: 978-1-4497-9224-4 (sc)
ISBN: 978-1-4497-9225-1 (e)

Library of Congress Control Number: 2013907107

Printed in the United States of America.

WestBow Press rev. date: 5/9/2013

TABLE OF CONTENTS

TEACHING

REBUKING

CORRECTING

TRAINING

DEDICATION

Sunshine and Delight

ACKNOWLEDGEMENTS

I owe great thanks to God almighty for the inspiration to write this book. I also owe a lot of thanks to Pastor Marshall Eizenga who was preaching the sermon the day God gave me the dream for this book.

A very big thank you goes to Apostle Aloy C. Diugwu for writing the forward to this book and for his friendship and for the many words of encouragements and prayers over the years.

I am also deeply grateful to Scott, Ikenna, and Faith who read the manuscript and for helping me make some necessary corrections. Worthy of mention is also my very good friend Great Chukwuemeka who reviewed and provided feedback for the initial manuscript.

Thanks to my publishers for working with me on this project and to all my destiny helpers who sowed financially into this project. May the Lord God almighty reward you all greatly in Jesus' name— Amen!

FORWARD

There are books and there is a book. Walking The Tight Rope is a book that every serious minded Christian should read.

The book is full of inspirations and divine directions.

In as much as Christianity is like a race, there must be a way to run it. There must be rules to be maintained, and some to be avoided in order to arrive well.

In that case, this book is a must read. You cannot read the first checkpoint and will not like to read the second checkpoint.

I recommend it for all.

Apostle Dr. Aloy C. Diugwu
Power To Reign Evangelistic Ministries Inc.

INTRODUCTION

The four checkpoints of the Christian profession

The goal of our walk with God is to stay in tune with Him for all time and eternity. He wants us all to be with Him in paradise forever. He wants all His Children to come home to heaven, at the end of our days here on earth. But as it were, many of us, if not all of us, are disobedient to His plan either all the time or from time to time. We have our own agenda, our own plans. We see things differently. And many times, we want nothing to do with Him at all.

The scripture tells us that *'There is a way that appears to be right, but in the end it leads to death.'*—Proverbs 14:12. As another scripture rightly says, *'we all, like sheep, have gone astray, each of us has turned to our own way;'*—Isaiah 53:6. Yet, God, in His infinite mercy and love, made a way for us—not willing that any should perish (2 Peter 3:9).

He is fully aware of all that is going on with us even when we think He is some distant landlord. He is still very close to us; He is even closer to us than our own breath. He is that friend that sticks closer than a brother (Proverbs 18:24). He made plans for us in His will every step of the way to make sure that there is always a way for us to come back to Him. God is love and in Him there is no darkness at all. His love compelled Him to make adequate plan for us all (Ephesians 1:8). This plan includes forgiveness of sins, redemption and eternal life. They are a complete package and accessible to anyone who believes.

Now for us to attain His desire for our lives, we have to undertake a journey or a walk of faith. Enoch was an excellent example as someone who walked close with God. The scripture records that he was not allowed to experience death but was transfigured to a celestial body and was taken up to heaven alive as a testament to his faith and obedient walk with God (Hebrew 11:5).

Now, for us to attain this level of spiritual maturity, we have to go through one or more of the four checkpoints below. This is true every day of our lives, and it doesn't really matter how long we have been believers or followers of Christ.

Someone could be in just one checkpoint at a time but it is also very possible to be in two or more different checkpoints at the same time. Someone might be in one checkpoint in a particular phase in his or her spiritual life and in another checkpoint in another phase. That is to say, it is very possible to be in a teaching checkpoint in one spiritual principle but also in a training checkpoint in another spiritual principle at the same time.

Be that as it may, it is almost a given that you will always find yourself in any one or more of the following checkpoints. The goal is to be on the training checkpoint in all phases of our spiritual lives.

What are these checkpoints being referred to and what does each checkpoint represent?

Before answering those questions, let us first take a look at the scriptural verse upon which this book is based (and we'll come across it time and again throughout this book). *"All Scripture is*

God-breathed and is useful for teaching, rebuking, correcting and training in righteousness," 2 Timothy 3:16

So, here are the checkpoints:

1. Teaching—new to the things of God or in a particular spiritual principle and being taught about faith towards God.
2. Rebuking—have been taught about the things of God but strayed from the Truths we had received and practised and are being rebuked or reproved. Or a blind spot we weren't aware of before.
3. Correcting—having been rebuked, we are now making amends and/or making restitutions
4. Training—'Walking The Tight Rope' on the narrow road. Galatians 6:1 describes the people on this checkpoint as 'those who are spiritual.' 2 Timothy 2:2 describes them as "reliable people".

Throughout the rest of this book, we will explore each of these checkpoints in more details, please join me.

PRE-CHECKPOINT

Scripture is our example

The reason God gave us the scriptures is to teach us—those who do not know, the ignorant, the unlearned and the simple—from the examples of the patriarchs or those who believed ahead of us. We all, at one point or the other, were alienated from God. We were strangers to the things of God and non-partakers of His divine nature.

We were all ignorant of the things of the Spirit and were by nature, children of disobedience subject to doom. But God so loved us . . . so much so that He gave us His Son, Jesus Christ, to die in our place as a propitiation for our sins. And for those who heed the call, the Apostle Paul writes '*God was in Christ reconciling the world to Himself*'—2 Corinthians 5:19. When John the Baptist walked the face of the earth, he preached and said, '*repent for the kingdom of Heaven is at hand*'—Matthew 3:2.

Then before Jesus ascended into heaven, He gave us the commission to preach the kingdom of God to every creature (Matthew 28:19) . . . . Now, the reason for this was because He does not want anyone to perish, rather He wants all of us to be saved (2 Peter 3:9).

This is why He inspired the holy men of God through whom we got the Holy Scriptures to write to us this wonderful love letter called the bible which contains His plan for the salvation of mankind. Brothers and sisters, no word of God is without effect or purpose. This is why we read in 2 Timothy 3:16 that *"All Scripture is God-breathed and is useful for teaching, rebuking, correcting and training in righteousness . . ."*

The reason or purpose He did this is expressed in a very concise term in the very next verse:

17. *". . . So that the servant of God may be thoroughly equipped for every good work"*

Listen friend, God wants all of His children to be ready for all good works. He wants us equipped for anything and everything the world throws at us and more importantly to be equipped for His kingdom. Make no mistakes about it, we wrestle, but it is not against flesh and blood. Our battle is against invisible spiritual beings in high places (Ephesians 6:12). For this reason, God does not want us to be unprepared. Rather, He wants us to be fully equipped for battle. And we understand that there is enough supply in God's armoury for the spiritual battles of life (Ephesians 6:11).

If, therefore, we suffer any casualty as we engage in these Spiritual battles, it will not be as a result of lack of the availability of Spiritual armours but as a result of our refusal to put them on. It even gets better; we understand that we are not fighting a battle we can ever lose. Jesus Himself tells us, to *'rejoice and be of good cheer . . . .'* In the face of trials and tribulations; in the face all the facts and fiery realities of life that we face every day; He says, *'rejoice and be cheerful.'* One could wonder why He would say that to us. Well, if you ever had that thought, here is His answer to you *'I have overcome the world'* (John 16:33). Remember we said that 'we are not fighting a battle that we can ever lose; For after He had won all spiritual and life battles by His blood, He gave us authority and says to 'occupy till I come'. Our job then is to maintain control and 'do business' until

His return. How else do we know all these things if we do not have His word living in us?!

Ephesians 2:10 introduces a new angle to this call to know Him *"For we are God's handiwork, created in Christ Jesus to do good works, which God prepared in advance for us to do."* This presupposes that we are not saved because we did something good or special; on the contrary, we have been saved and called to do the good works which have been pre-ordained for us. The duty of the entire scriptures then is to prepare us, teach us, rebuke us, correct us and train us to do these very works we have been called to do.

Nobody is saved or will ever be saved simply because he did something good, great or amazing. But everyone saved has been saved and called to do good works.

Just like in every job we do in life, we need some training. First, we were taught what is expected of us and we were sometimes supervised (rebuked and corrected—if that is what it takes) until we got the job done. Then after passing through the learning curves, we got to the point that we were expected to show some level of competency. And sometimes, we were expected to train others on the same job (2 Timothy 2:2).

Between Ephesians 2:10 and 2 Timothy 3:17 lies the essence of the whole scriptures. In Ephesians 2:10 we are called to do good works but to be able to do these good works we have to get to 2 Timothy 3:17—*thoroughly equipped for every good work*—we go through the whole scriptures from Genesis to Revelation.

Our main scriptural reference is 2 Timothy 3:16 and it outlines to us the purpose of the entire scriptures which is teaching, rebuking, correcting and training till we attain verse 17 status—'thoroughly equipped'. God does not want us to be ill equipped rather to be completely and thoroughly equipped for every good work.

These four key components presented in verse 16 are what we will be referring to as Checkpoints. If indeed any and every scripture is supposed to present one or more of these components to each one of us, then we need to pause every so often as we read through the scriptures to make sure that these checkpoints are being observed.

Before we plunge fully into the rest of the text, may I make a plea to you? If you do not know Jesus as your Lord and Savior, would you consider inviting Him into your heart right now? He died on the cross of Calvary as the propitiation for all our sins. The sinless Son of God was made sin so that the sinful man may become righteous before God (2 Corinthians 5:21). If anyone believes in Him that person has the promise of everlasting life (1 John 5:11). Scripture teaches that *"If you declare with your mouth, "Jesus is Lord," and believe in your heart that God raised him from the dead, you will be saved"*—Romans 10:9.

If you believe in Him, would you please pray this simple prayer with me, out loud? "Lord Jesus, I believe that You are the Son of God; I believe that You died on the cross of Calvary for my sins and was raised again from the dead for my justification. I gladly receive You now into my heart as my Lord and Savior—Amen.

If you said this prayer in faith, you are now born again. Find a bible believing Church and attend. Make sure to tell someone that you just became a Christian.

Dear friend, there is joy in heaven right now, all because of you!!! (Luke 15:10).

Now that we have this settled, let us explore the checkpoints together . . . .

TEACHING

My child, pay attention to my words; listen closely to what I say.

Proverbs 4:20 - 22
(NCV)

FIRST CHECKPOINT

Like newborn babies, crave pure spiritual milk,
so that by it you may grow up in your salvation—1 Peter 2:2

The first checkpoint is the entry stage; the infancy stage, if you will. Here we were first taught the word of God. Many of us embrace the word and follow it. God uses many things to draw us to Himself. He could use the words of a friend or a preacher or a chance tract on the road side. Well, not that He was unaware of the 'chance tract', but He provisioned that in His divine perfect will to be so. Yet for others, He uses special circumstances to bring us to Himself.

Many people come to the knowledge of our Lord and Saviour after some strange, yet divine encounters, others by an act of a miracle. There are many stories of people who had angelic visitations in their dreams. Many people from around the world where the preaching of the gospel was prohibited have reportedly come to the saving knowledge of Christ through some unique circumstances. Stories have been told of people who had visions of Jesus Christ Himself appearing and preaching to them in their dreams. Whatever the case may be, each of us has a story of our own encounter.

While this stage is typically thought of as the 'introduction to Christianity 101', it could also be applied to someone who was already a Christian. For instance, someone might be very knowledgeable in a particular spiritual principle but knows so little about another spiritual principle. When this person is first brought face to face with this new revelation, it always comes in the form of teaching.

We are always learning and developing and growing in our spiritual walk. Take Moses for instance. He was someone attested to have seen God 'face-to-face' as it were, yet he needed his father in-law to teach him 'delegation of authority' (Exodus 18:13-27).

We also read in the Acts of the Apostles where a group of believers were instructed by Apostle Paul on the gifts of the Holy Spirit. These people were obviously followers of 'the way', as Christians of those days were called, but were not aware of this very important Christian principle.

In their own words when asked ". . . *did you receive the Holy Spirit when you believed?*" replied, "*No, we have not even heard that there is a Holy Spirit.*" This was the opportunity Apostle Paul ceased to teach them about the baptism of the Holy Spirit. The entire story is recorded in Acts 19:1-7. The same could be said of Apollos when Priscilla and Aquila met him as recorded in the Acts of the Apostles chapter 18:24-28.

Here are a few things we learnt about him in verse 25:

❖ He had been instructed in the way of the Lord
❖ He spoke with fervor
❖ Not only that he taught about Jesus but there was another qualifier here—he taught accurately!

The scripture was also careful to tell us what he knew

❖ His knowledge was limited only to the baptism of John

One great lesson here was that he wasn't ready to be limited by his apparent limitations. He was willing to push the envelope. He was willing to thread where others dreaded. He was willing to take on the establishments and all opposition from the authorities. He did not claim to posses all knowledge, but he was willing to exercise a 'training' level walk of faith while still open to a 'teaching' level walk of faith. We will see later how Priscilla and Aquila played the role of teachers as 'trainers' in this spiritual walk phase.

Teaching

Jesus was referred to as the Rabbi or Raboni which being interpreted means—The Teacher. His entire earthly ministry could be categorized as teaching. He did not teach just by words but by works as well. In fact, when Luke wrote his dear friend Theophilus in Acts chapter 1 verse 1, he was explicitly clear that what he wrote in his first book (gospel according to Luke) was about *"all that Jesus began to do and to teach."* In other words, Jesus demonstrated that what He was teaching or was about to start teaching was, as a matter of fact, doable. He demonstrated that by first doing them and then teaching them. The order is very important.

There are several ways we could teach others. There are several strategies. Scripture tells us about Jesus *'He did not say anything to them without using a parable . . .'*—Mark 4:34. The Great Teacher knows best. He knew how to reach the people and He used illustrative stories to drive home His teaching. He told several parables about money, servants, farmers, good neighbor, hidden treasures and rewards.

He used stories the people of the time were very familiar with. The stories themselves did not require so much explanation. Although the morale of the stories may be higher than the average person on the street could easily comprehend, He made sure it was a story they themselves could relate with. Then from what they knew, He gently led them to what they ought to know.

Sometimes He would bring them in on the story by asking them to provide an answer or draw a conclusion, like the parable of the Good Samaritan (Luke 10:25-37).

Exploring the First Checkpoint—Strategy for Teaching

❖ The great commission
❖ Creating the environment
❖ Winning the lost at all cost
❖ Discipleship

The great commission

Preach the word; be prepared in season and out of season; correct, rebuke and encourage—with great patience and careful instruction—2 Timothy 4:2

The great commission is a clarion call for all believers in Christ Jesus. In giving this great commission in Matthew 28:19-20, Jesus commands all believers to ' . . . go . . . make disciples . . . . teach them to obey . . . .' This is not one of those works we leave for only the televangelists, pastors and church leaders. On the contrary all and sundry are called to participate in disseminating the gospel of the kingdom of God. If there is one thing guaranteed, it is that His presence will always be with us. As someone once said, 'those who know do; those who understand teach'. Jesus wants us to both know and understand the spiritual principles so that we may also impart it unto others (2 Timothy 2:2).

Now, nobody is expected to stay on the teaching checkpoint for a life time; at least not on the same. However, there are those who are supposed to be teachers already but are still requiring to be taught the very same spiritual principles (Hebrews 5:12). And there are also those who are always learning but never able to come to the knowledge of the truth (2 Timothy 3:7). This is not what is expected of us as Christians, rather we ought to learn, grow, then be able to teach others.

We understand that the most dangerous water is the stagnant water. It harbours all kinds of diseases and deadly infections. But a stagnant spiritual life is even worse; not only does it lead to all kinds of spiritual sicknesses but it also leads to a stunted spiritual growth. What happens here is you find someone who is able to recite several scriptural verses without any spiritual depth or understanding.

That person ends up criticizing every other believer who is experiencing blessings locked up in the scriptures that the stagnant believer was not able to unlock. Meanwhile the scripture clearly teaches that only the scriptures we understand and act upon will work for us (Matthew 13:15). In other words, we can only unlock a scriptural blessing by understanding and acting accordingly in agreement with what God is saying to us in that portion of the scripture.

We have to learn and practice this principle; then when we see the positive results in our own lives we are encouraged to teach others the same.

Every teacher, on the other hand, is encouraged to give oneself to in-depth study of the scriptures. This does not only help us communicate our ideas clearly to our audience but also helps us gain approval from God.

One of the most important things taught in public speaking is being knowledgeable in the subject matter and this, I can say, might have been learnt from the Holy Scriptures (2 Timothy 2:15).

You may not know everything there is to know, but you will need to know enough to know that there is more to know. You will be knowledgeable enough to be willing to yield yourself to the Spirit of God to fill and pour you out to others.

We are not really called to be experts. If we were, I wouldn't be writing this piece. I don't consider myself an expert in any way, but I understand that God is able to use anyone. I also understand that availability supersedes ability. This is why in spite of all my weaknesses and frailties, I have decided to yield myself to the Holy Spirit of God for His use. Didn't the scripture say *". . . do not worry about what to say or how to say it. At that time you will be given what to say"*—Matthew 10:19—I will therefore, most gladly, yield myself and let God use me.

Starting from the very moment I got the burden to write this book and said yes to the Lord, He has provided the guidelines and words for His people. Edward Foggs of Westbow publishing rightly said to me 'the moment God gave you this book idea, He had people lined up to read it otherwise He wouldn't give you the book idea'. I couldn't agree more with him.

Jesus once said and still says the same today *"He who is not with Me is against Me, and he who does not gather with Me scatters . . . ."*— Matt 12:30. This simply means that nobody should ever claim to be sitting on the fence. We all have to be engaged one way or the other. Ron Kenoly in one of his songs puts it this way ". . . there is no demilitarized zone; you are either on the Lords side or on the devil's side . . . ." This is therefore my own little way of engagement and pouring out some of what I have learnt over the years. I want to encourage each of us to get engaged. There is no room for complacency (Amos 6:1). Each of us should be learning or exercising what we have already learnt by living it out and teaching others also.

Creating the environment—at home, work and play

Let your conversation be always full of grace,
seasoned with salt, so that you may know how to answer
everyone—Colossians 4:6

Without any fear of equivocation, the hardest place to teach or preach is at home. Many people would easily pick up their bibles and preach to a total stranger, but at home, you are weighed against your teaching or preaching. And Jesus wants us to be thorough and complete. Not just appearing holy to strangers and then something entirely different at home.

Just before Jesus ascended to heaven in Acts 1:8; He told His disciples to be His witnesses starting from Jerusalem. Jerusalem, we know, is their capital city and He wants them to start right at home. Charity, they say, begins at home. He wants a complete well rounded people of God. Those who would live what they preach or teach.

The Apostle Paul on describing the qualities of a bishop says that a bishop should be 'one that rules over his own household' (1 Timothy 3:12). We ought to be able to put our houses in order. The four checkpoints of our Christian profession principle suggest that while we might still be struggling in one area, we might be excelling in another. The key then is to keep working on those areas that need to be worked on while perfecting those areas we are already strong at until we get ourselves to the training checkpoint in all areas of our spiritual lives.

Though we might not all get to that spiritual level before we are taken up in glory or before Christ's second coming, we will be blessed if we remain faithful to the call (Matt 24: 46). The blessing is not because we have finished the work, but because we are found at our duty post—doing what the Word says.

Now, while we do the work of the evangelist, we ought to know that folks don't like being preached at. People want to be shown that they are loved and cared for. The Apostle Paul in one of the scriptures mentioned that he is everything to everyone that if by any means he could win them to Christ.

We saw that approach played out in Acts 17:16-31. He did not go all out to condemn the Athenians for their idolatry; although one might say that he barely stopped short of doing just that. What he did rather, was find a way to initiate a conversation which would lead many to the saving knowledge of Christ.

Let us look at his interaction with them on that occasion.

First of all, we noticed how distressed he was about the level of idolatry in that part of the world, but he found a way to use their own words to preach to them about the living God. Verse 28 was the key here. He had taken time to learn about the people, and had quickly learned some of their poems. The event described here might have happened over a few days so that he had time to study the people and their culture. It might also be possible that he just learned about the people and their culture on the go.

The important thing here, however, is that he was very observant to have listened to and recognized the words of their poets. One way of showing people that you really care about them and what they are going through is by remembering what they had discussed with you—their names, their peculiar situations and circumstances.

It is not usually enough to say 'am praying for you', but we could do more and try to remember what it is we are praying for them about and communicate that to them. Call them by name or even a pet name that is unique to them and announce to them that we care and so does our God.

The people Paul was meeting with were people who discussed the latest and greatest ideas. They were by no means ordinary minds. They were what we would normally describe as great minds. However, Paul was wise to refer them to the poems by their own poets. He chose to start from what they knew and were familiar with to what they didn't know but ought to know. From one of their poems, he chose the phrase "... we are His offspring ...." From these four little words he segued into what would become a great sermon. 'If so be that you claim to be His offspring, how then do you think that He is a piece of silver or gold or wooden idol?' Here are his very words in verse 29 *"Therefore since we are God's offspring, we should not think that the Divine Being is like gold or silver or stone—an image made by human design and skill".*

With these and many more words he preached to them the gospel. After that conversation, we would read this in verse 34 *"Some of the people became followers of Paul and believed. Among them was Dionysius, a member of the Areopagus, also a woman named Damaris, and a number of others."*

What can we learn from here? Firstly, we learnt that the Apostle Paul did not preach at the people. And secondly that he found something from the people's literature which the people could relate with that he could use as an offshoot for preaching the gospel to them. And lastly that great harvest of souls followed. I personally believe that he yielded himself to the leading of the Holy Spirit.

I had previously struggled with trying to convince people to believe in Christ Jesus. You see, for me it was really easy to believe in His love, compassion, grace, miracles and plan for the salvation of mankind. It was so easy for me that I wondered why others just couldn't believe as easily as I did.

I also had another struggle sharing my faith with people I would normally consider as 'good people'. And I have met quite a few people under this category that would pass ordinarily as good people. Or at least I would consider them as good people. And for that reason, I found it difficult to start sharing the gospel with them.

For both struggles the question I had was the same, "how do I start?" I don't want to appear awkward and I definitely don't want to come across as throwing the bible at people. I just want to be as normal as normal can normally be, but at the same time, I want to be able to preach the gospel, for '... woe is me if I do not preach the gospel.'—1 Corinthians 9:16 (NKJV).

Well, after a series of studies and prayers, I found that I could use the Pauline principle. Find what is common with a particular audience that could be used as a bridge or segue to bring in the salvation conversation and while at it, endeavor to communicate the message of eternal life (1 John 5:11). Let them know that God gave us eternal life, but this life is in Christ, such that the only way to get into this eternal life is through Christ.

I met this young man who would later become one of my best friends. At the time, he wasn't a believer in Christ Jesus.

He was one of the smartest kids in our class then but he had such an attitude that made me less likely to want to be around him. Although I was already a Christian, I just couldn't bring myself to the point that I really wanted to preach the gospel to him. And this is not necessarily due to his behavior at the time but due mainly to the fact that I wasn't ceasing all the opportunities that were presenting themselves for me to use to share the love of God with him.

I remember one day I had said the name of Jesus out loud and he asked me why I was saying that name and I simply responded 'out of the abundance of the heart, the mouth speaks'.

I admit that the way he asked me the question and the way that I responded were not exactly the friendliest of ways. I know that I could have done better. And that was an opportunity for me to tell him that Jesus saves and that I have been saved and also to ask him if he would like Jesus to save him too. But I failed.

Well, not long after that, another person found a good opportunity and preached the gospel to him and he believed. Now he is waxing strong in the Lord and preaching the gospel to many too. He is also in the ministry in his local Church in Newcastle England. Sometimes I ask myself, 'how would it have felt to have led him to Christ?'

Well, I had another opportunity slip through my hands again. I met someone who helped me find my way when I newly arrived in Canada. We exchanged our contact information and stayed in touch for a while. Sometime later, she needed help and I was happy to assist. To me, it was an opportunity to pay her back in some way for her kindness to me when I was missing my way. All I did was offer the help that was requested; nothing more, nothing less. Again I did not preach the gospel to her.

One day my phone rang and it was my dear friend on the phone. She has found Christ (not that He was hiding or anything like that, but that someone else had preached the gospel to her and she believed.) Now, if you were me, you'd be asking yourself why you were off to such a slow start with so many missed opportunities.

Although she told me one day 'though you did not preach the gospel to me, I knew that you knew God from the way you live your life.'

Sometimes, I find myself trying to analyze the situation and try to determine who is more likely to believe or not. Well, I can say right now that that was then. I try to cease any opportunity I see now. Although the person doesn't really have to believe at the moment, yet I really have to preach. I have learned that "no one is responsible for making anyone believe, but everyone is responsible for telling someone that Jesus saves." When we do our job, God does His job—what only He does best—conversion of souls.

One other day, I met this young man whose house was just a few blocks from mine. I said to him, 'I'd like to stop by someday'. He agreed on a date and time and I showed up as planned. Well, I had only one thing on my mind. 'Preach that word!' After sharing the gospel with him, I asked him if he had any questions. I was sure he would have some gazillion questions. But to my surprise he had none. Well, that wasn't the first time I was wrong and I don't even think it would be the last time I'll ever be wrong.

He gave his life to Christ and before long was out there preaching the gospel. In those days, among my friends, we called him 'Big man'. He had a speech impediment but that would all be gone when he went out preaching. I was so proud of him.

There was also this young man that went to the same secondary school as I did. We always went to his class to preach the gospel after which we'd invite the students to a student fellowship on campus. He would not come to our school fellowship that was held after school for fear of his parents. But I was very surprised when he came up with another smart reason he would not attend the fellowship held once a week during recess.

A few years later, I was the hostel captain and he had been sent to live in the hostel by his parents. Of all the hostels and of all the empty bunks there were, he was sent to my hostel and he chose the very next bunk to mine.

In those days, no student wanted to be close to the prefect's bunk and definitely no junior student wants to stay that close to a senior student let alone the prefect. And the prefects themselves want their own little extra space.

I enjoyed all that space until one day I came back and saw that the empty bunk right next to mine has been occupied. I demanded to know who 'dared' occupy my extra free space and do you know who showed up? Leonard! That was the name of the new boy. I was going to ask any other student to leave and find another space, as there were many other free spots, but not this new kid. "Where is your Christianity?!" One would have rightly asked.

Well, long story short. We were two years apart . . . that means that my last year in school was his first senior year. He was a very smart kid and had written an exam to attend a special science school for his senior secondary school years and had passed. I expected him to accept the offer and be gone. But much to my surprise, he came back to our school (Union Secondary School) for his senior years. When I asked him why he came back, he asked me 'who would take care of the fellowship when you are gone?'

In those days he was one of my 'school sons' but I did not expect him to take over that responsibility. I knew God will always take care of His work. But Leonard would not listen to me. He stayed back and carried on with leading the fellowship after I had graduated.

The last time I saw him after graduating from the University, he was already a pastor. Halleluiah! The fruit remained and is bearing fruits to eternal life. Lord, may I never miss another opportunity to preach the gospel to the lost! We know that it is the Holy Spirit who convicts people and not us. Our duty then is simply to preach the gospel in season and out of season—whether it is convenient to us or not. There is a perfect division of labor here. We preach it, He confirms it. Someone plants the seed, another waters the seed, but God is the One who makes it grow (1 Corinthians 3:6)

Winning the lost at all cost—being all things to all people

... I have become all things to all people so that by all possible means I might save some—1 Corinthians 9:22

Sometimes to save some people will require us to lay down our own lives. We read in John 3:16 that the love of God to us through Christ was fully expressed by Christ going to the cross and laying down His life for us, what is even more interesting is that 1 John 3:16 has this to say *"This is how we know what love is: Jesus Christ laid down his life for us. And we ought to lay down our lives for our brothers and sisters."* It is a mirror verse for us to emulate the example of Christ.

The apostle Paul made an amazing statement which could not be said in any better way. In 1 Corinthians 9: 19-23 he said these words:

Though I am free and belong to no one, I have made myself a slave to everyone, to win as many as possible. To the Jews I became like a Jew, to win the Jews. To those under the law I became like one under the law (though I myself am not under the law), so as to win those under the law. To those not having the law I became like one not having the law (though I am not free from God's law but am under Christ's law), so as to win those not having the law. To the weak I became weak, to win the weak. I have become all things to all people so that by all possible means I might save some. I do all this for the sake of the gospel, that I may share in its blessings.

It is very important to observe here the reference to different groups of people. This scripture is not by any means suggesting that the Apostle lived like them to the extent of imitating their life styles in order to reach them. However, as we saw in Acts 17, there is a strong reason to believe that he studied them and as someone else said 'spoke the language of the Babylonians' to be able to reach them.

The time this section was written was a time in the US history that some 20 innocent children and about 6 brave teachers were un-provokingly murdered at their place of learning in Newtown, Connecticut. This led to so many debates on the television about the US gun laws. Now, to talk to someone intelligently on this matter would require you to know the statistics about what is on the ground and then finding a scriptural backing that will help you bring comfort and consolation to the people and as well to persuade the government to think differently about their gun laws.

Just quoting the scriptures to an unsaved and untrained mind might not be enough sometimes, but if you can 'speak their language'; If you can show them from their own statistics how gun related crimes is on the increase in the advanced countries and correlate that to the decline in moral education among youths. Then you might have an ear when you say *'Direct your children onto the right path, and when they are older, they will not leave it'*—Proverbs 22:6.

We ought to find a way to reach the people without sounding so out of touch with reality. We shouldn't be too heavenly conscious that we become earthly useless. We need to be able to rejoice with those who rejoice and mourn with those who mourn (Romans 12:15). When we relate with people, we have a better chance of reaching them for the Lord.

Our greatest example is Christ. We saw Him not only visiting people some religious leaders would term as 'sinners' but He was also eating with them. One of them was Matthew who would later write the gospel book by that name. We should never write anybody off. Our responsibility is to preach to 'every creature'.

Discipleship—living the preaching or teaching

Whatever you have learned or received or heard from me, or
seen in me—put it into practice—Philippians 4:9

Discipleship is not as easy as preaching and teaching. By discipleship you are letting your life do the teaching for you. Doctor Luke in Acts 1 tells us that Jesus *'began to do and to teach'*. It is very imperative that we observe the order He carried out His earthly ministry; He did, then He taught. This is the most powerful and effective way of teaching.

As people come to faith, they are often referred to as children. Now we know that the most effective way children learn is by observation and imitation. They look at the adults and do as they did. We saw Jesus being invited by some communities after performing some miracles to stay with them a few days.

In John chapter 4, we saw the Samaritans ask him to spend some days with them after the conversion of the woman at Jacob's well. This gave them the opportunity to observe Him up close. He doesn't just have to tell them to pray, they'll see Him pray and when He tells them to pray, they know He does what He teaches. In Luke 11:1 we saw that it was after the disciples saw Jesus pray (which I believe was His routine) that they demanded *'Lord, teach us to pray'*. He taught them by examples—practical living examples.

We also saw the Apostle Paul in 1 Corinthians 11:1 make a profound call *"Be imitators of me as I imitate Christ"*. This is a powerful statement. In other words, don't just do as I say but do as I do. Not only are we encouraged in Hebrews 13:7 to closely observe the outcome of the life choices of those who teach the word of God to us, we are also enjoined to imitate their faith. And Jesus also warned His audience against those whose lives are in direct contrasts to their teachings (Matthew 23:3).

Indeed, in the great commission in Matthew 28:19, Jesus did not just ask us to preach and teach but to make disciples. A disciple is someone who follows someone or studies someone. Almost like an understudy. A disciple is one who would someday be like the mentor. This level of preaching requires a total submission to God to control our everyday life.

We know how we react when we are driving along the other driver that cuts us off on the traffic or the guy who refuses to drive past the traffic light when it was clearly green. Sometimes you can almost tell they were on their cell phones texting and weren't paying attention.

Sometimes you are almost sure the person was just chit-chatting with the person on the passenger seat. You know how impatient we can grow sometimes and honk the horn at them and yell and scream. Some people even swear at other drivers. Have you realized that most times when you finally go past that other driver, that they are almost always older people or younger people that we might consider as 'learners'? Imagine you had a disciple by your side watching your actions and reactions. Many people have different reactions depending on who was around.

Let it be known today that we are called to be life mentors. We are supposed to make disciples of all nations. We teach the word not just in words but also in actions or deeds. The Apostle Paul challenged his audience to emulate his life style. He threw the same challenge to the Christians at Ephesus as he did to the Corinthians, the Philippians, the Thessalonians, and the Hebrew Christians.

We saw the challenge about ten times to be followers or imitators of his examples. 1 Corinthians 4:16; 11:1; Hebrews 6:12; 13:7; Philippians 3:17; Ephesians 5:1; 1 Thessalonians 1:6; 2:14 and 2 Thessalonians 3:7 and 9—all these scriptures clearly show a life that was lived out in full view of his audience.

They were well aware of his 'conversations' or way of life. For this he could confidently say, *'imitate me as I imitate Christ'*. This is the life we are called to live as those who would disciple others for Christ. We are called to be the ambassadors of Christ (2 Corinthians 5:20).

REBUKING

". . . My son, do not make light of the Lord's discipline, and do not lose heart when he rebukes you . . ." Hebrews 12:5.

SECOND CHECKPOINT

*Brothers and sisters, if someone is caught in a sin, you who live by the
Spirit should restore that person gently. But watch yourselves,
or you also may be tempted—Galatians 6:1*

Rebuke is not necessarily a harsh reprimand or sharp
criticism for something done wrong. It should be done
purely out of true love and in the spirit of meekness. The
purpose is not to hurt the person whom the rebuke is directed at but
to restore such person to fellowship with God and the Holy Spirit.

Revelation 3:19 (KJV) states it this way *"as many as I love, I rebuke
and chasten: be zealous therefore, and repent."* The purpose of
rebuke is stated clearly in that simple verse. God wants us to do two
things: 'to be zealous' and 'to repent'.

To be zealous in this context simply means to remember our first
love—The things we were taught originally and had embraced
(Revelation 2: 4-5). To be enthused about the call we had received
and to express hunger for more of God. To repent then, simply means
to give up our current thought process and actions and go back to the
God approved way of living.

So, when we find ourselves at this checkpoint in our walk with God,
it generally means that we had learned some spiritual truths but had
gone our own way to live our lives in a way contrary to the standard

of God's word (2 Timothy 2:19) and for that are being rebuked or reproved.

Sometimes we are rebuked by the scriptures. The apostle James described the scriptures metaphorically as a mirror. In James 1: 23-25 the role of the word of God as a mirror is to point out our errors and flaws and for us to take the rebuke of the Lord and amend our ways.

When someone is alive in the spirit, that person is always sensitive to the nudging of the Spirit of God and is aligned with the Spirit's leading and can quickly respond to the rebuking from the word.

But other times we are reproved or rebuked by the brethren who are aware of our way of lives or whose lives might have been affected by our actions or in-actions (Matthew 18:15) and sometimes we are rebuked by a word of prophesy during a congregational fellowship or worship.

King David was one who was rebuked by Nathan the prophet for his behaviour in Uriah's death. The same could be said of Apostle Peter when Apostle Paul withstood him and rebuked him for an act of hypocrisy.

One can also consider the look that Jesus gave to Apostle Peter as a type of rebuke after Peter had denied knowing Him three consecutive times at His trial before the crucifixion.

Just like in the first checkpoint; some rebukes are not necessarily that we have gone back to doing those things we know are not part of our calling. Sometimes it could be a blind spot where we don't even realize we are sinning and needed correction. Other times also, we are simply ignorant of the truth and needed someone to point it out to us. We saw two times in the epistles of the Apostle Paul where we were cautioned against ignorance, "*I will not have you ignorant*", he said (1 Thessalonians 4:13 and I Corinthians 10: 1). Sometimes ignorance could be such a deadly disease.

In 1 Corinthians 3:16 he wrote the following words *"Don't you know that you yourselves are God's temple and that God's Spirit dwells in your midst?"* Sometimes, people need to be reminded what they already know or ought to know. As a matter of fact, sometimes, we need to hear certain things over and over again especially when our lives are not reflecting our professions.

In communicating to the Hebrew Christians the Apostle Paul wrote in the following manner *"are not all angels ministering spirits sent to serve those who will inherit salvation?"*—Hebrew 1:14. Although one might not immediately see this verse as a rebuke or a reprove, however, it is easy to deduce that the author is speaking to a group of people that should know the subject he was discussing and is in a sense reprimanding them for acting as if they did not know.

If he were to be teaching this spiritual truth to people who were not familiar with that principle, he would say something like this *"all angels are ministering spirits sent to serve those who will inherit salvation"* but putting it as a question or rather a form of a rhetorical question, it clearly shows that he was talking to those who should know and in a way calling their attention to that truth that they are most likely not actualizing in their lives.

Rebuking then is not always for an error of commission but could sometimes be for an error of omission.

Exploring the Second Checkpoint—Strategy for Rebuking

- ❖ Rebuking others
- ❖ Being rebuked by others
- ❖ Dealing with push backs
- ❖ Maintaining relationships

Rebuking others

> *My brothers and sisters, if one of you should wander from the truth*
> *and someone should bring that person back, remember this:*
> *Whoever turns a sinner from the error of their way will*
> *save them from death and cover over a multitude*
> *of sins—James 5:19-20*

Nobody likes to be rebuked. The natural man wants to feel loved and appreciated but nobody really wants anyone to point out his or her errors. It takes a lot of humility to accept that one's ways need to be amended.

Scripture tells us that no rebuke or reprimand seems pleasant at the time it was given. But we shouldn't stop there; let us look at the rewards that follow thereafter. *"No discipline seems enjoyable at the time, but painful. Later on, however, it yields the fruit of peace and righteousness to those who have been trained by it"—Hebrew 12:11.* Here we can clearly see the rewards—Peace and righteousness. The reward far outweighs the present feeling we get when our actions are disapproved.

That being said, one very important thing for the person rebuking others to realize is that there is a scripturally approved method for rebuking someone else. The language of rebuke is 'meekness and love'. We already established from the scriptures that no one likes to be rebuked, nevertheless, we have to. Now, since we have to, there has to be a way to do it. And that is the way of love.

Someone once said "there are two ways to say anything, and one of them is, 'kindly'". Someone might be wrong but our attitude while rebuking them will determine how receptive or rejecting they will be toward us and towards the rebuke.

Let us study 2 Samuel 11 and 12. In chapter 11 we saw King David do the unthinkable. Scriptures tell us clearly that the Lord was not pleased with David. I mean, he was wrong in more ways than one. He committed adultery, cover up, conspiracy, murder, you name it. He was as guilty as charged and more. God already confirmed that in the very last verse of chapter 11.

God had to send a prophet by the name Nathan with the details of King David's sins and he had come to rebuke the king for his errors.

How did Prophet Nathan handle this message from God to David? Some will approach David with a holier-than-thou attitude. Some will shout it at the roof top. Some will announce it in prayer meetings in the pretence that they want to solicit prayers for the brother or sister 'who had sinned'.

Is there any scriptural example for us to follow in dealing with this type of situation or even when someone had done us wrong? First of all, Matthew 18:15 teaches us to first go to the person that offended us and try to settle the matter with the person separately without involving any other person.

Now, let us see how Nathan handled this matter. Chapter 12 of second Samuel has all the answers. First of all he went to David with a parable. He found a subtle way to get King David's honest reaction to the situation and painted him a picture that he can clearly relate with.

He spoke about animals, of which King David was not a stranger. He spoke about the closeness of the animal and its owner. King David in writing Psalm 23 clearly demonstrated a clear understanding of what it means to lay down one's life for his cherished animal. He then put in a little twist. He likened David's cravings to 'a stranger'. And at the end of the narration, King David had a verdict—Death to the culprit.

Well, isn't that our attitude most of the time? As long as it does not involve us, we are okay with whatever happens to other people. But Nathan was different; his rebuke was in love. His intention was neither to condemn the King nor to have something over him. No! He showed the attitude the Holy Scripture advocates in Galatians 6:1. His mission was that of restoration not condemnation. We see that clearly in verse 13 "... *the Lord has taken away your sin* . . . ."

Unlike Jonah who refused to take the message of love to the people of Nineveh but ran to Tarshish instead (although that plan was thwarted by God—Jonah 1-4) for fear that God would relent from sending them a 'deserved punishment' for all their evils and iniquities, Nathan went with a heart of love and was happy to see that David truly demonstrated a mark of true repentance.

The apostle Paul in writing two of his sons in the ministry clearly instructed them to rebuke those who err. This will help them to correct their errors and get back in fellowship. In 1 Timothy 5:1 and 2 we read the following "*Do not rebuke an older man harshly, but exhort him as if he were your father. Treat younger men as brothers, older women as mothers, and younger women as sisters, with absolute purity*"

The charge in the above verses was not to 'never rebuke someone', but to do so with kindness. He used the word 'exhort' which means to 'strongly encourage or urge (someone) to do something'. This supports our earlier statement that a rebuke or reprove could be equally applied to an error of omission as well as to an error of commission.

However, in verse 17 through 21 we saw both commendation or recognition and rebuke. Those who do well are supposed to receive both honor and financial support while those who are sinning should be rebuked or reproved in the presence of others. The reason for this was so that others might learn.

We are also warned against partiality or prejudice. If anybody is to be rebuked, it must be out of pure love and its goal must be to make the subject a better person, overall. In Titus 1:13 the Apostle Paul teaches that one of the many benefits of a firm rebuke is that it makes the one who receives it sound in faith. This spiritual exercise is not an avenue for carnal 'showmanship' or for getting even with someone. Anyone with such attitudes should not engage in this all important spiritual adventure.

Being rebuked by others

Open rebuke is better than secret love—Proverbs 27:5

It is not always the same feeling when we are on the receiving end of any rebuke. Our natural instinct is to kick against it, to fight back. We want to protect our ego and defend our positions. We feel our guard is being let down and others are talking to us 'anyhow'. We put up this wall to fend all 'intruders' off. I mean, 'who do they really think they are?!'

Well, whenever we have this attitude, it is a sign of a more serious and deeper underlying problem. We falsely think we are above mistakes and therefore above any form of reprove or rebuke. And sometimes, we look at the person trying to admonish us and question what or who gave them the impetus or effrontery to talk to us. Some people might even go to the level of denigrating the brother or sister who dares to admonish them; sizing them up based on their educational and/or societal status.

It is even harder when our friends think it was time they pointed out our faults to us. We give them the 'et tu Brute' response. But the scripture in Ecclesiastes 7:5 clearly states that "*It is better to heed the rebuke of a wise person than to listen to the song of fools.*" Why so? Well, the answer is simple, '*wisdom preserves those who have it*'—Ecclesiastes 7:12.

Now, let us look at the attitude of King David to Prophet Nathan's rebuke. The first part of verse 13 of the 12th chapter of the second book of Samuel contains one of the most profound confessional phrases in the entire scriptures "*I have sinned against the Lord*". In that simple statement, David accepted his sins and also the verdict that he gave for the perpetrator when he did not know he was the one.

We know that much because in the very next sentence in the same reference above Nathan responded by saying "*The Lord has taken away your sin. You are not going to die*". King David was both remorseful and repentant. We can clearly confirm that the mind of the prophet and indeed that of God is not to condemn us in our sins and short comings but rather that we may hear His rebuke and repent of our sins (Revelation 3:19).

But why is it important for us to accept rebuke from others when we have fallen in our Christian walk with God? Scripture was very clear when it warned us against the deceitfulness of sin (Hebrews 3:12-13). If we are not rebuked or reproved, we soon become complacent and hardened.

There is a grave danger for those who were once 'enlightened' when they go back and return to their former life-style (Hebrew 6:4-7). We are to watch out for ourselves and for one another (Hebrews 3:13)

WALKING THE TIGHTROPE | 31

Dealing with push backs

"You don't know what you are asking," Jesus said to them. "Can you drink the cup I am going to drink?" "We can," they answered—Matthew 20:22

There are times you approach someone with their faults or failings and you try to put it the nicest way you know how to and all you get is a push back. They are not really interested in what you are all about or what you are trying to say to them. You can almost feel they have already made up their minds about the situation and are not willing to bulge one bit.

If you like, bring all the scriptures in the whole wide world and all the 'thus says the Lords'. What do you do when you get push backs? How do you react to push backs and still reach your objective of helping someone on his or her spiritual journey? Are there indeed, scriptural references that can help us deal with these types of situations?

There are 5 steps outlined in the scriptures as a model to restoring a believer from error:

1. If someone offends you and returns and says forgive me, forgive him (Luke 17:4)
2. If they did not come to you, go to them and show them the error of their ways, if they repent forgive them (Matthew 18:15; Luke 17:3)
3. If step 2 fails, take one or two more persons with you and go talk to him/her, if they repent, forgive them (Matthew 18:16)
4. Take the matter to the Church if step 3 fails (Matthew 18:17)
5. And finally when all else fails, treat the person as an unbeliever (Matthew 18:17)

Matthew 18:16-17 has the laid down Christian way of dealing with push backs. Step one is to increase the number of witnesses (Verse 16). Remember that your initial approach was to go all by yourself and talk to the erring person. If the person gave you a 'Davidic' response, then your work is done and there will be joy in heaven over such a soul.

But the Holy Spirit clearly shows us that some people's response might be less 'Davidic' than we would anticipate and hence laid out for us the step by step guide to dealing with push backs.

When we get the initial pushback, the response from us is to take one or two more believers with us as we approach the erring person. The criteria for selecting these one or two more persons are stated out clearly in Galatians 6:1—they have to be spiritual and meek; not 'radio without batteries' nor 'town crier wannabes'.

Nobody wants their issues to be left in the open. We have to be careful in selecting whom we talk to concerning our matters with other believers. When these criteria are fulfilled and we have approached the brother or sister with whom we have a matter to settle, we have a better chance of winning such person or persons back and covering a multitude of sins (James 5:19-20).

The next step if the above fails will be to take the matter to the Church. This is the last and highest level we wish to go as Christians because if all else fails at this level, we are confronted with a very frightening outlook—The person will be treated as an unbeliever.

This simply means the person has just become another 'mission field'. We are not expected to hold them to the same spiritual standard as other believers again. We should still love, care and pray for them but we should also know that they are not believers and should relate to them as such.

Maintaining relationships

How good and pleasant it is when God's people live
together in unity!—*Psalm 133:1*

The fact of the matter is that no matter how spiritual we are, we are still living in a body and sometimes there are conflicts and misunderstandings. This is almost a given, so we are not going to spend so much time here. Our effort is rather going to be focused on what we would do to heal the wounded or broken relationships after the fact.

In the process of rebuking and trying to point out other people's flaws, we might stretch it so thin that we would have conflicts of interests. The scripture verse in Acts 15:39 stated that a sharp disagreement ensued between Apostles Paul and Barnabas over John who is also called Mark.

The King James Version of the bible described it as a 'sharp contention'. We remember how that the Holy Spirit had said earlier in verse 2 *"Set apart for me Barnabas and Saul (who would later be called Paul) for the work to which I have called them."*

Now, who would have thought that these two men whose works were clearly ordained by the Holy Spirit Himself would ever face conflict of any kind? I mean, if there is any perfect setup, theirs' is one already. The power of the God-head had given His sign of approval, He called them out by name and they were prayed for, committed to God and sent forth. The problem or issue that brought the contention was another fellow that accompanied them during their first missionary journey. A disciple by name John also called Mark.

We found in verse 5 of the Acts of the Apostles chapter 13 that John Mark went with them as a helper. But somewhere along the way, he bailed on them and returned to Jerusalem. This was why during their second missionary journey, the Apostle Paul advised against taking him with them again to avoid a repeat incidence.

If you thought the first missionary journey was tough, wait until you wake up in jail with hands and feet bound in fetters of iron and chains and the only thing allowed to move without chains was your mouth. And Paul and Silas did use those to bring down the presence of heaven (Acts 16:25-26).

The last was not heard about these men. Though Paul and Barnabas parted ways and moved on with separate missionary partners, they were quickly able to resolve their differences and their relationships were healed. We know that this was, as a matter of fact, true because Paul wrote to the Corinthian Christians in his first epistle chapter 9 and verse 6 *"Or is it only I and Barnabas who lack the right to not work for a living?"* This clearly is not the statement of one who is still nursing grudges against his fellow minister.

We can go one step further to say that their reconciliation was complete to the point that John Mark was later considered as a helpful fellow in Apostle Paul's missionary work such that when Paul was writing Timothy in his second epistle, he wrote *"Only Luke is with me. Get Mark and bring him with you, because he is helpful to me in my ministry"*—2 timothy 4:11.

How do we know that these statements were not made before the conflict? Well, we are certain because Paul did not meet with the disciple called Timothy until Paul and Barnabas had parted ways (Acts 16: 1). So, not only was the relationship between Paul and Barnabas healed, but also that of him and Mark the disciple.

There has to be a secret that enabled these early disciples to deal with misunderstandings and conflicts. We have already established that as people living in the flesh, we are bound to have some conflicts from time to time. The question now is 'how do we deal with such conflicts when they do arise?' The Apostle Paul himself declared in Ephesians 4:26-27 *"In your anger do not sin: Do not let the sun go down while you are still angry, and do not give the devil a foothold."*

Someone who proclaimed about ten times "be imitators of me as I imitate Christ" must be confident that he indeed practiced what he was preaching otherwise the people of the time would point this out to him. I kind of believe that the conflict was resolved shortly after they had it as the Holy Spirit bore witness to their ministry both in jail and at the jailors house.

To maintain relationship after a dispute, conflict or disagreement, we have to learn from the Apostle Paul himself. In Acts 27: 10-11, his advice was scorned by the captain of a ship. The result was a massive loss and painful journey. However, in verse 21 he reproves or rebukes them. But he didn't end there, from verse 22 to 26 he provides encouragement and brought them a prophetic word about their journey. They did not all agree at the beginning but he too did not go all out to tell them it was 'all-their fault'. He found the right balance between rebuke and comfort and gave them just about the right dosage.

I could find no better illustration to conclude this section than the story of Father Abraham and his nephew, Lot. Maintaining relationships sometimes could be proactive rather than reactive. We should identify areas in our relationships that are prone to causing conflict between brethren and try to resolve them before they got worse. Most conflicts always start small. Our ability to identify them early and nip them in the bud is a testament to our spiritual maturity.

Do you know that sometimes, abundance could carry its own problems? Abraham and his nephew Lot were both wealthy men. The Lord had blessed them with livestock, silver and gold. But the problem they had was rather a 'good' problem. They had the problem of lack of space to keep all their belongings. Both men had servants and herdsmen that took care of their livestock. In verse 7 of Genesis 13 we were told of the reported quarrelling that arose between the herdsmen of both men.

In a proactive and mature manner, Abraham identified the problem and concisely states the matter to his nephew. Now, although Abraham was a much older person than Lot, he was not mindful that Lot would choose the choice land ahead of him. Verse 8 to 11 describes the approach Abraham adopted to resolve the conflict. The reasoning behind his decision to resolve the conflict was captured in this five word phrase ". . . for we are close relatives . . ."

This phrase quickly brings to mind and echoes the very words of the psalmist when he said *"How good and pleasant it is when God's people live together in unity! It is like precious oil poured on the head, running down on the beard, running down on Aaron's beard, down on the collar of his robe. It is as if the dew of Hermon were falling on Mount Zion. For there the Lord bestows his blessing, even life forevermore"*—Psalm 133:1-3.

Where there is peace and unity, there is prosperity and life. When we learn to forgive one another and live in peace with one another, blessings are bestowed and we have a taste of heaven here on earth.

CORRECTING

". . . . but whoever looks intently into the perfect law that gives freedom, and continues in it . . . will be blessed in what they do"—James 1:23-25.

THIRD CHECKPOINT

For though the righteous fall seven times, they rise again, but the wicked stumble when calamity strikes—Proverbs 24:16

Correcting is the third checkpoint of our Christian profession. This is for those of us who have learned and practiced the word of God but have strayed from the truth and were rebuked or reproved, either by the Word of God or by fellow believers, and have repented of our ways again and are now willing to make amends and come clean with God.

We find King David such an awesome example of this checkpoint. Psalm 51 was written by King David after the rebuke he received from Prophet Nathan. We saw a man with a broken and a contrite heart. The bible tells us that God will not overlook such a man. After the rebuke, we found King David in such a sincere repentant mood; he came to God with an honest plea to restore to him the joy of salvation.

Dear friend, there is no true joy for the sinner, and it is even worse for a backslider. King David understood this truth, which is why he pleaded earnestly with God not to take away the Holy Spirit from him. We know that the Holy Spirit is the seal; the sure proof of our salvation and we also know that He, the Holy Spirit, guarantees our fellowship with the Father and the Son. But when we walk away from God, we lose the communion of the Holy Spirit and our fellowship with the Father and the Son is broken. This is such a dangerous place to be! The way out is to quickly come back to God in a true heart of repentance and beseech Him diligently to mend our fellowship with Him.

In the synoptic gospels, we found Peter weeping earnestly as a sign of true repentance from his ways (Matthew 26:74-75; Mark 14:72; Luke 22:61-62). It was this same Apostle Peter that we read in Acts 5:29-30 "*. . . We must obey God rather than human beings! The God of our ancestors raised Jesus from the dead—whom you killed by hanging Him on a cross.*" He spoke boldly in the presence of great multitudes about Jesus whom he had previously denied when only a small crowd was present. This must be an evidence of true conversion.

Jesus had said to Peter before the denial, "*. . . But I have prayed for you, Simon, that your faith may not fail. And when you have turned back, strengthen your brothers.*"—Luke 22:32. Stories had it that at the end of his life he was crucified for his faith, upside-down.

Many of us, every day of our lives, come to this checkpoint many times, some probably a little more than others. But this is not one of those checkpoints that we want to stay on, for the same reason, for a very long time. And as often as we visit this checkpoint for various and different reasons, as we mature in our spiritual walk, we are encouraged to quickly '*make straight . . . a highway for our God*' and get back to fellowship. Because "*we know that anyone born of God does not continue to sin*"—1 John 5:18.

We are encouraged to live a life devoid of sin. However, if and when we do sin and are rebuked or reproved either by the scripture or a fellow believer, we ought to quickly repent and get back to fellowship.

John the beloved apostle admonished us this much when he wrote and said "*My dear children, I write this to you so that you will not sin. But if anybody does sin, we have an advocate with the Father—Jesus Christ, the Righteous One*"—1 John 2:1

Exploring the Third Checkpoint— Strategy for Correcting

❖ Acknowledging error in one's ways
❖ Taking the steps back
❖ Receiving help from others
❖ Helping those on their way back

Acknowledging the error in one's ways

I will set out and go back to my father and say to him: Father, I have sinned against heaven and against you—Luke 15:18

The first step in making amends and correcting ones errors is by acknowledging that something was indeed wrong and needs to be changed. It starts by first reflecting on what has been done wrong and what should have been done or not done and trying to find a bridge between the gorge of what is and what ought to be.

It starts with self assessment and an understanding of what is required of one in that particular circumstance. A typical example we can draw from is the parable of the prodigal son in the gospel book of Luke chapter 15.

The first thing we can tell about a backslider or someone who has gone away from the faith is expressed in verse 13. And that is: that person has gone to a far country. Secondly, that person is squandering the father's love and wealth. Worse still, that person will soon come into a very big need or want.

We are spiritual beings that live in earthly bodies and one of the most important needs of our lives is spiritual intimacy. When that is not there, we have this insatiable hunger in our lives that neither drugs nor any other forms of addictions satisfy. Many feel this form of void and emptiness in them and find themselves looking for solutions where there is none. You can't get spiritual satisfaction from a therapist! You need to come home.

The void we feel when we stray from God is 'God-sized' as some preachers say. And this can only be filled by God and God alone. We could try other options but we will always fail, guaranteed! Why do you waste your time on something that can never satisfy? (Isaiah 55:2-4)

'What is the solution then?' One may ask. Well, the answer is in verse 17. But before putting down the verse here, may I quickly say that every sinner is *'out of his or her senses.'* We see many amazing promises in God's word as outlined by the psalmist in Psalm 91:1 *"Whoever dwells in the shelter of the Most High will rest in the shadow of the Almighty"*. The rest of the verses of psalm 91 are full of divine promises of long life, provisions and protections. One would think that no one would ever want to leave such a shelter—the Presence of the almighty God. Well, if you do think that, then you are either naive or don't really understand human beings. We want to exercise that God-given freedom of choice and many times we choose what is clearly not in our best interest(s).

Going back to our text in Luke 15:17 *"When he came to his senses . . . ."* now you see what we were talking about. Although he was acting 'all smart and wise', he was actually out of his senses. At this point he realized how much he was missing by being away from home. 'Oh! What peace we often forfeit, only because we do not carry everything to God in prayer!' the song writer says.

The rest of the parable portrays the joys that followed his conversion and return home. Heaven threw a grand party for him. He was dead and now alive; he was lost and now found (Luke 15:24.) Similar thing happens among the angels each time a wanderer comes home.

King David was such a man after God's heart and there are so many scriptures to attest to that, but let us just look at Psalm 51 again. After Nathan's rebuke he did not start giving excuses neither did he start denying the alleged offences. He simply opened up to God in true repentance. *'Surely I was sinful at birth, sinful from the time my mother conceived me'* he said. He was referring to man's fallen state and helplessness by virtue of our birth. He realized how helpless he was and knew that no therapy could help him but God's Spirit. He earnestly asked God not to take the Holy Spirit from him. It is a dangerous place to be anywhere without the abiding presence of the Holy Spirit of God. Please, be reconciled to God! (2 Corinthians 5:20)

Remember that making corrections does not necessarily mean changing a life of sin. It could be an area of the spiritual life that we are ignorant of and had practised in ways that gave us less than God's 100 percent for our lives and the scripture or someone points it out to us. We saw in Acts 19, that when the disciples were told about the gifts of the Holy Spirit, they instantly received the message by faith and were all baptised in the Holy Spirit. We also saw the same effect with Apollos when Priscilla and Aquila invited him to their home after they had heard him speak the Word of God and explained to him the way of God more adequately and he went with more knowledge and proclaimed the Word with boldness and with fervor (Acts 18:26). The result that followed spoke volumes about the 'correction' provided by Priscilla and Aquila. Their role here was pointing out a blind spot in Apollos' ministry which he accepted whole-heartedly and took the necessary 'training exercises'. The result speaks for itself. He became a very great help to other believers (Acts 18:28). In fact, he became so influential that some people wanted to identify themselves with him. The Apostle Paul would later write ". . . One of you says, "I follow Paul"; another, "I follow Apollos"; another, "I follow Cephas"; still another, "I follow Christ"—1 Corinthians 1:12. What a transformation?! He became very great to the point that he was reckoned among the gospel greats.

Taking the steps back

*Consider how far you have fallen! Repent and do the
things you did at first . . . .—Revelation 2:5*

So after acknowledging one's error, the very next step is taking the
first step back. The journey of a thousand miles always begins with
a step. In fact, the very first step tends to be the very most important
steps of all.

Someone once said '*not knowing and not knowing that you do not
know: that is foolishness; but not knowing and knowing that you do
not know: that is wisdom.*' The only reason someone would want to
take steps back is if that person truly believes that he or she has gone
far from home.

I have had so many people tell me how far 'home' was from 'where
they were'. And I have always wondered how many of them actually
realized that their 'home' never moved but they did. You see,
whenever we feel far away from home, it must be that one of two
things has happened. It is either that we moved or that the home
moved. But since the home would not normally move by itself, it will
be logical to conclude that we must be the ones that moved. This is
the same with us and God. Whenever we feel God is so far away, we
must be the ones that moved from His presence.

Jesus says, *"All those the Father gives me will come to me, and
whoever comes to Me I will never drive away"—John 6:37.* So, if
He will never drive one away, then we must have willingly walked
away. The prodigal son in Luke 15 did. However, we saw that when
he came back to proper reasoning, he took the necessary steps to
amend his ways. Verse 18 tells us what he did. He said to himself '*I
will set out and go back to my father . . .*' In other words, he decided
and determined to do something about it.

This is not just wishful thinking; he actually did something about it. Remember he was not being coerced or forced in any way by someone preaching at him; although his circumstance was doing much more than that for him already. But more than just saying I will set out and go back, he rightly identified where he had fallen from—he had fallen from grace and fellowship with the father.

The very next thing he says is very crucial, *". . . and say to him . . ."* the healing process most times starts with saying something. The ministry of reconciliation is a ministry of words. We start by saying something. He understood the words of Hosea the Prophet which says "Take *words with you and return to the Lord. Say to him: 'Forgive all our sins and receive us graciously, that we may offer the fruit of our lips'"—Hosea 14:2.*

Even though righteousness is by faith (believing in the finished work of Christ on the cross), salvation comes only by confession. It is important that our meditation and confession agree, however, it is only by our confessions that we are justified or condemned (Matthew 12:37).

Whether it is sin or a particular area of weakness that we are struggling with, whether it is a new course we are trying to chart or reclaiming a promised land, the approach to obtaining victory is the same. We have to confess the words of faith. The Apostle Paul wrote *"It is written: 'I believed; therefore I have spoken.' Since we have that same spirit of faith, we also believe and therefore speak"*—2 Corinthians 4:13.

The prodigal son understood this principle also. Now, before going any further, it is very important to remember that the parable of the prodigal son was an illustrative story used by Jesus Christ to demonstrate the heart of God toward all His erring children. This is the mind of Christ for us: 'to be reconciled to God' (2 Corinthians 5:20). When we follow the same examples, we obtain the same results.

Receiving help from others

. . . But that is not what God desires; rather, He devises ways so that a banished person does not remain banished from Him—2 Samuel 14:14

Most times, we are the ones that actually know how we hurt or where we need help. It is our responsibility then to speak up and speak out. *'Let him that thirst come'* (Revelation 21:6; 22:17; John 7:37; Isaiah 55:1). In Matthew 11:28, Jesus issued a command saying, *'come to Me, . . .'* but that call was for the *'. . . weary and burdened . . .'* and the reward is *' . . . rest'.*

Notice how the call is an open call. The weary, the burdened, the thirsty has to know that he or she is thirsty and reach out to the fountain. Sometimes we just have to initiate the move and ask for help. As the Apostle James rightly puts it *"confess your sins to each other and pray for each other so that you may be healed. The prayer of a righteous person is powerful and effective"—James 5:16.* The sins referred to in this verse imply weakness or shortcomings. When we are weak and need help, we should look for other believers with proven integrity and ask them to assist us to get back to fellowship with the Father.

But then again, there are those times that people come to us either by word of knowledge or revelation and offer to assist us. These people have been instructed by the Holy Spirit to provide support and counsel. The Ethiopian Eunuch in Acts 8:26-40 was approached by Philip and asked if he understood what he read.

We saw in verse 26 that the angel of the Lord had clearly instructed Philip to go near the Ethiopian, who obviously needed help. His case was not returning from an error of his ways but getting over a mountain of ignorance. He was reading the book of Isaiah but had no clue what or of whom the prophet was talking about. Doesn't that represent most of us? There are so many things we don't understand, we have so many questions and we hope that one day, just one day, and maybe when we get to heaven, we will have all the answers.

The Ethiopian could have kept to himself and lived on with his ignorance. He didn't have to tell Philip anything. Remember he was an important government official. He was the treasury secretary of his country. But hear him in verse 31 *"How can I (*understand what I am reading*)," he said, "unless someone explains it to me?"* So he invited Philip to come up to his chariot and sit with him.

Sometimes we just have to invite others to come up to 'our chariots' to sit with us and help us through our journey or we simply get down 'our chariots' and demand help. This wise Eunuch did both (Acts 8:31; 36-38)

When the Apostle Paul encountered Jesus on his way to Damascus, he knew that he must stay with those who were believers before him to help him grow. Both in Damascus and in Jerusalem, he made sure his main companions were those who were believers already (Acts 9:19-29). He knew the importance of godly companionship. He would later write *"Do not be misled: 'Bad company corrupts good character'"*—1 Corinthians 15:33.

As we make our way back, we need to be mindful of the company we keep. I still remember my first day at secondary school. At the school gate, my Dad had said to me 'Ogbom (meaning 'my name sake' in Ibo dialect. Both of us share the same first name—James), I know you will not join bad groups' to which I responded 'yes sir'. Well, every other decision or choice I ever made till this date was based on that brief 'truth moment'.

My father understood what influence company could have on anyone. At least, he was much older and he is someone I would describe as 'been there; done that' and I was not going to experiment to find out if he was right or wrong. I took it from him and swallowed it hook, line and sinker. Well, that was actually why I became a born-again Christian. I made a preacher in my class my best friend. The reason was simple; I figured there is no way 'this one could be a bad group'. Dad was right, although he passed on shortly after that. I graduated among the best in my school, had all the awards, represented my school in many academic competitions and never 'got into trouble' any day.

2 Samuel 14 has the story of the estranged son of David, Absalom. Verses 28 to 33 demonstrate the passion of someone who wants a restored fellowship with his King. Absalom sought the help of the King's right hand man, Joab, to bring him back to his father, the King. Joab then used all the tricks in the playbook to get the kings attention and to bring his son back to the kingdom. Verse 33 concludes this way ' . . . *And the king kissed Absalom*"

This was somebody the King didn't want to set his eyes on ever again (2 Samuel 14:24). Yet when Joab intervened, the king changed his mind. Listen brothers and sisters, even if you think your case is so bad that there is no way to make it back, we have an advocate with the Father, Jesus the righteous. He pleads and mediates for us (1Timothy 2:5).

Helping those on their way back

Now instead, you ought to forgive and comfort him, so that he will not be overwhelmed by excessive sorrow—2 Corinthians 2:7

I have heard some preachers talk about 'vision helpers'. These are people that help others fulfill their visions. They are not the ones that received the original vision but they are willing vessels to help the persons with the vision fulfill their mandate.

Likewise, on our way back to fellowship with God, we have such people to help us every step of the way. Jesus said to Apostle Peter in Luke 22:32 ". . . *when you have turned back, strengthen your brothers . . . .*" Anyone who has had any form of experience dealing with a particular situation is better situated to help someone currently going through similar circumstance. As a matter of fact, we owe a responsibility to one another to watch out for fellow believers and are commanded by the scriptures to ".... *consider how we may spur one another on toward love and good deeds*"—Hebrew 10:24.

When someone is making amends in his or her walk, it is important the words we speak to them. It is important that we are not too critical in criticizing them. In fact, our job is to admonish and encourage (Ephesians 5:19). Being too critical has the effect of discouraging someone from trying.

Jesus knew all about Peter's future denial yet He looked beyond that to see an Apostle with great oratorical power that can turn five thousand unbelievers into strong disciples in one meeting. He did not put Peter down for his apparent act of cowardice, when he denied Him in the presence of a little girl, rather He instructed him to encourage other believers when he is restored.

It is also important that we do not flog a dead horse. That someone was wrong by omission or commission at one point or the other does not necessarily mean that they will always do the same thing over and over again. We should learn not to describe people by their apparent weakness(s). Even though Peter was weak and acted cowardly, Christ called him Peter (Rock or stone.) After the resurrection their conversation was not centered on Peter's denial (during His trial) but on a future ministry he must fulfill. Peter's response captured it this way, his weaknesses notwithstanding "*Lord, you know all things; you know that I love you*" to which Jesus responded "*Feed My sheep.*"—John 21:17

Jesus Christ is the greatest teacher of all time and what we can learn from Him here is that He does not condemn anyone because that person was weak or wrong; rather, He offers rest to the weary and we ought to do the same (Matthew 11:28)

TRAINING

"For physical training is of some value, but godliness has value for all things, holding promise for both the present life and the life to come"—1 Timothy 4:8.

FOURTH CHECKPOINT

But solid food is for the mature, who by constant use have trained themselves to distinguish good from evil—Hebrew 5:14

The fourth Checkpoint is the training stage. We will call this checkpoint 'Walking The Tight Rope'. There are several keywords or phrases that stand out in the key verse for this checkpoint (Hebrew 5:14), and one of such phrases is 'by constant use', another one is 'trained themselves'. Constant use presupposes the individual involved is making a conscious effort to go back for more of the word. This type of believer is presented to us in Acts 17:11.

They are the noble Christians who constantly examined the scriptures to confirm the certainty of the teachings they had received. They might not be leaders of great congregations but they sure do understand the meaning of Colossians 3:16 *"Let the message of Christ dwell among you richly as you teach and admonish one another with all wisdom through psalms, hymns, and songs from the Spirit, singing to God with gratitude in your hearts."* This verse of the scripture urges us to 'Let', or 'allow', or 'permit', the word of Christ to dwell in us not just sparingly but richly. These trainers have first trained themselves (Hebrew 5:14) and are now in a position to train or mentor others.

This is where we want to be every day till Christ comes. This is what Jesus was referring to when He said, *'occupy till I come.'* Another translation puts it this way: *'do business . . . until I come back'—Luke*

19:13 (New English Translation). This is the position Apostle Paul wants us to take when he said, '. . . *having done all to stand, stand therefore . . . .*' We are expected to be alert here. We are supposed to be super vigilant and watch over our own souls. There is no time to be at ease. There is no room for laxity. We should always be sober otherwise, we could go astray. This is a constant everyday thing for us to do. We have to be aware of the antics of the enemy. But more importantly, we have to know the mind of God towards us in all circumstances.

This by no means suggests we should be paranoid and fearful that we may stumble and fall. That is far from it. The Scripture in Jude verse 24 tells us that God is able to keep us from falling. We are guaranteed that the eternal God is our refuge (Deuteronomy 33:27). There is no greater assurance than this. Anyone who believes in Him would never be shaken nor moved (Isaiah 28:16). Our ability to stand or resist temptation does not come from our physical or mental strength; it comes from God's power. As the Apostle Peter rightly articulated it in 1 Peter 1:5 '*we are being kept by the power of God unto salvation*'. Our call and duty then is to maintain our ground.

Yes we know the road is strait and narrow; and yes we know that there are many uncertainties there, yet we know that God has promised to see us through. Those of us who are walking this rope are also expected to bring others in. We are expected to train others. We are expected to pull them as if from the fire, if that is what it takes. We are encouraged that we are not alone. We are encouraged to persevere for there is a crown for us if we do not faint. Scripture is full of promises for those who turn many to righteousness—they will shine like stars (Daniel 12:3).

Here, just as in the preceding three checkpoints, we have identified four specific sub-checkpoints to consider.

Exploring the Fourth Checkpoint— Strategy for Training

* ❖ Mentorship—Maintaining the spirit
* ❖ Running according to the rule
* ❖ Being under constant check
* ❖ Enduring till the end

Mentorship

A mentor is a beacon of light for others to look up to. Mentors inspire great aspiration in the lives of the mentored. This role is what the mature Christians are called to fill. And to do this, they are expected to give themselves to the study of the word of God, prayer and fasting. Those in the training stages are not only spiritually mature but are able to train themselves and able to train others also. They are those described in Hebrews 5:14 as able to eat solid spiritual foods. They are those who, themselves, have '. . . exercised . . .'

Look friends, to be a personal trainer in life requires the trainer to be in top physical shape. So also a Spiritual mentor ought to be in top Spiritual shape.

Let us rethink about Paul and Barnabas for a moment. After their split over John Mark, Barnabas took Mark as his companion while Paul left with Silas for their respective missionary journeys. After this time, little was heard about Barnabas and Mark but we did hear about Paul and Mark sometime later. This could only mean one thing. Mark's life has turned around so much that Apostle Paul would personally demand him to be brought to him. He wasn't considered as a spiritual dead-weight any longer but a valuable companion.

Well, while we are still on the subject of Mark being such an awesome valuable companion, let us not forget that he received spiritual mentoring from no less of a mentor than Apostle Barnabas himself. His name, by the way, actually means 'Son of consolation, son of exhortation, or son of comfort' (Acts 4:36). Barnabas is much like a character builder. We could say he is a personal spiritual trainer. Barnabas almost single-handedly, with the help of the Holy Spirit of course, changed the person of John Mark we saw in the first missionary journey in Acts 13:13 to the on-demand spiritual character we saw in 2 Timothy 4:11.

Scripture teaches that *". . . No one who puts a hand to the plow and looks back is fit for service in the kingdom of God"*—Luke 9:62. What then does this say of John Mark? He turned back from the missionary work. Was he now unfit for the kingdom? Well, we already saw in 2 Timothy 4:11 that the Apostle Paul clearly stated ". . . Get Mark and bring him with you, because he is helpful to me in my ministry'. What really happened between the first missionary journey and this time that Paul was writing? All that we know from the scriptures about Barnabas and Mark was their family relationship (Colossians 4:10). But knowing that Barnabas is an encourager or a life coach and that both of them embarked on a missionary journey together, we can conclude that Barnabas poured his life into this one soul.

We knew from the first missionary journey that Apostle Paul was the chief speaker (Acts 14:12); we could probably conclude that Paul was more of a public speaker while Barnabas did more of other ministry training. This showed clearly in the transformation that took place in the life of Mark afterwards.

Today, we do not know of any epistles or gospels written by Barnabas the Apostle, but we sure do have the gospel according to Mark. Moreover, we see that Paul mentioned Mark in several other epistles of his. This is a sure testament to the impact Apostle Barnabas had on him. This is the work a mentor is called to do; inspire others to overcome their weaknesses and limitations to the point that they are able to train and mentor others. We are trained to be trainers. Although Mark would have been deemed unfit for the kingdom, Barnabas walked him right back to the point where he could be counted among the gospel greats.

Jesus said to the Apostle Peter "*when you have turned back, strengthen your brothers.*" In other words, be a mentor to other believers. Let them learn from you that being down does not automatically mean they should be out. Let them know, from your life testimony, that they can rise up again and be outstanding for the kingdom of God. Dear friends, true mentors are those who set examples for their followers in speech, in conduct, in love, in faith and in purity (1 Timothy 4:12).

Running according to the rule

Similarly, anyone who competes as an athlete does not receive the victor's crown except by competing according to the rules—2 Timothy 2:5

There is an expectation for someone who has 'come of age' in terms of spiritual growth. Their life becomes an epistle for others to read. They are being held to a higher standard than the 'average Joe'. I once read a book in my secondary school days called 'where there is no doctor'. These believers could be called 'where there is no bible', because they are indeed, living epistles for all to read (2 Corinthians 3:2).

Jesus teaches that a city on a hill cannot be hid. These believers are cities on hills with flood lights on them. Their lives echo the grace and mercy of God. In the call for the great commission, Jesus challenged his followers to go and 'make disciples' of all nations. He didn't say to just preach the gospel; He challenged us to make disciples. That term as we saw earlier, simply means to let their lives do the preaching. Jesus the greatest Teacher began to do and to teach;

we his followers ought also to do and then teach; or simply put, 'let our actions do the teaching.'

People are tired of teachers and preachers with head knowledge alone. They are interested in those who would let their lives do the teaching. The world is almost challenging us to stop telling them how to be believers and start showing them how to be believers. The reason we see many secular people challenge our profession today is because many of us are full of words without works. Jesus teaches that His followers should be able to do the very things He did and even more. He acknowledges that some will believe without seeing any signs but also that some would really need to see some signs to believe. While there is more blessing for the former, we are also encouraged to demonstrate God's awesome power to all the doubting Thomas's.

"If you don't believe my words, believe for the sake of the works," Jesus says—John 10:38. This is the calling for the trainer. Not just being a 'nominal' believer, but a true believer: one who showcases the amazing power and presence of God in his or her daily life. We saw that one of the criteria for choosing the Deacons in Acts 6:3 was 'full of the Spirit' and 'wisdom'. These are demonstrable and tangible qualities. And these qualities are very important to the Apostles because these believers were soon to become mentors or spiritual beacons for others to look up to. Let me just quickly say here that if it was very important to them then, it is still very important to us today. The need has never been more nor are the stakes higher than this day and age that the Christian faith is being challenged by claims that we know are false scientific knowledge (1 Timothy 6:20).

We have to live above the fray and demonstrate the power of the God who has called us. A believer in this class is someone who understands the power of the gospel to convict sinners in the error of their ways. And to put the doubters in their rightful position—shame.

We saw this style demonstrated by the Apostle Paul in Acts 13:6-12 when he preached the gospel of our Lord and savior Jesus Christ to an important government official, Sergius Paulus. A magician tried to confuse the official and distract him from the message of salvation.

Many of us today will give in to political correctness or false humility. But not one who is running according to the rules. Not one who understands the power of the gospel. The apostle Paul announced to him *". . . Now the hand of the Lord is against you. You are going to be blind for a time, not even able to see the light of the sun."* Dear friend, the impact of that statement was instantaneous. We would read in the second part of that verse *"Immediately mist and darkness came over him, and he groped about, seeking someone to lead him by the hand"* Acts 13:11. Upon witnessing this epic show-down, Sergius Paulus did not need any further lengthy sermon to convince him of whose power is the ultimate power. No wonder scripture says, *"Thy people shall be willing in the day of thy power . . ."*—Psalm 110:3 (KJV).

While the Christian profession encourages everyone to come as is, it promises to transform the life of anyone who comes in faith. You may come as you are, but you are not allowed to remain the same. You do not make your own rules, no! There is a standard. 2 Timothy 2:19 clearly admonishes those that call on the Lords name to live a life worthy of their calling. And it is even a lot more than that. Aside from us claiming to belong to the Lord, is the Lord Himself claiming to belong to us?

That same scripture above tells us without mincing words that *"the Lord knows those who are His."* And the Apostle Peter tells us that God is no respecter of persons. In order words, God does not show favoritism but accepts anyone who lives righteously (Acts 10:34-35).

In Acts 19:13-16, we saw a clear demonstration of '**what not to do**'. Some men who clearly have not 'trained themselves' in this spiritual principle went and engaged in exorcism and got the beating of their lives. They wanted to demonstrate the 'acts' of Apostle Paul without first taking his 'spiritual training exercise'. They served as a good deterrent for those who would afterwards contemplate such attitudes.

To be a trainer then requires constant training. The King James translation of the key verse of the fourth Checkpoint reads as follows *"But strong meat belongeth to them that are of full age, even those who by reason of use have their senses exercised to discern both good and evil"*—Hebrews 5:14. The key word here being EXERCISED! Now, when athletes are getting ready for competitions or championships, they do not normally start with the most difficult drills, do they? Of course they don't. They normally start with something small and work their way up to their target. So also is the spiritual exercise.

We have to start from somewhere and make our way up; each one of us at our own pace. There is really no competition here. What you cannot do is 'do-nothing'. Find one spiritual exercise and engage in it and move up from there. We are transformed from glory to glory (1 Corinthians 3:18).

One catch phrase we hear from athletes or personal trainers these days is 'if you don't use it; you'll lose it'. How true is that statement to us today in terms of Spiritual exercise?! This brings us to the next subtopic: Being under constant check.

Being under constant check

Be alert and of sober mind. Your enemy the devil prowls around like a roaring lion looking for someone to devour—1 Peter 5:8

It doesn't take so much for people to become complacent. Getting used to something sometimes has some disadvantages. We sometimes

WALKING THE TIGHTROPE | 61

forget to retrain ourselves. We think we can always get it done anytime. We got used to knowing how to pray that prayer becomes a routine mental exercise. We have so rehearsed our prayers that we don't even think about the words we say. We become too familiar with God and the words we use in prayers. Soon, if we don't keep ourselves under check, we start sounding arrogant with our hands in our pockets while we issue commands to God with some deadline ultimatum.

I have heard people say some horrible things in the name of prayers. 'God, if You don't do such and such things for me at such and such time I will throw away my bible and stop believing in You'. To some, there is totally nothing wrong with this attitude towards God in prayers. 'Afterall, bible says to pray at all times and in every circumstance'. But if we do not watch this type of behavior, it will eventually lead us to a dangerous slipping slope into 'Sampsonism'. Sampsonism is a spiritual state where one is not aware that the Spirit of God is no longer with him or her although they could still speak those Halleluiah languages. They are simply having the form but not the power (2 Timothy 3:5).

By the way, if you are one of such people that always 'threaten' God with throwing away your bibles and stopping to believe in Him, repent of that lifestyle right now and ask the Holy Spirit to lead you into all truths. God is not moved by our 'threats'. Or don't you know that our unbelief does not nullify God's faithfulness (Romans 3:3).

The way to keep ones spirit alive and active at all times is by constantly examining one's life and making sure that it is still in agreement with the standard of God's word. Some people are trying in vain to lower the standard of God's word to meet their fallen standards instead of lifting their fallen standards to meet God's infallible Standard. God's firm foundation stands sure (2 Timothy 2:19).

How does one live a life that is constantly geared towards the standard of God's words? Since the life of a fallen man is incapable of meeting

God's standard, the only way we can achieve that standard then is by living a transformed life. This transformation does not come instantaneously, rather through a process of renewing of our minds using God's word so that we will be able to test and approve what God's will is—His good, pleasing and perfect will (Romans 12:2). When we do this, we are no longer spiritual babies being swayed by every doctrinal teaching; rather we will grow to become in every respect the mature body of him who is the head, that is, Christ (Ephesians 4:14-15). Then we will *"continue to live our lives in him, rooted and built up in Him, strengthened in the faith as we were taught, and overflowing with thankfulness . . ."*—Colossians 2:6-7.

The scripture goes one step further urging the believers to constantly *"Examine yourselves to see whether you are in the faith; test yourselves. Do you not realize that Christ Jesus is in you—unless, of course, you fail the test?"*—2 Corinthians 13:5. It is the constant examination that helps us stay connected to the Vine without whom we can do nothing (John 15:5).

Enduring till the end

But we do not belong to those who shrink back and are destroyed, but to those who have faith and are saved—Hebrews 10:39.

Our faith and hope in God is not in vain (Isaiah 45:19). He did not call anybody to follow Him just for the sake of it. On the contrary, there are abundant blessings for anyone who heeds His call. Scripture tells us that God rewards those that follow Him diligently (Hebrews 11:6).

Dear friend, our reward for the faith we have in God is two folds. Not only do we have rewards in this present world, but we also have eternal rewards in heaven for all eternity. 1 Corinthians 15:19-20 teaches us that much. When this present life is over, either through death or by rapture, we are promised resurrection and life everlasting.

The Christian profession is the only vocation that has no retirement. We are believers in life and in death. When we follow God diligently in life we are preparing for an eternal bliss in His kingdom. Although sometimes it seems we are being crushed and bruised, yet we know that it is working out for us an even weightier glory (2 Corinthians 4:17). All we have to do is endure to the end; as the scripture says, "... *but the one who stands firm to the end will be saved....*"—Matthew 24:13.

Doesn't it strike you that the scripture did not say, "but he who stands firm the longest?" nor yet, "but he who stands firm through the hardest and toughest circumstances of life?" You see, the emphasis is on "the end", seeing it through. Not starting and quitting when the going gets tough. God did not promise us a trouble-free life, but He did promise to be with us through the waters and the fires and through all the storms that life throws at us (Isaiah 43:2).

The book of revelation is full of verse after verse of encouraging words for the believer to endure to the end **(Revelation 21:7; Revelation 3:21; Revelation 3:5; Revelation 2:26)**. He that overcomes will receive crowns. My dear brothers and sisters, Jesus has already overcome for us and given us victory, all we need to do is to maintain our territory (1 John 5:4-5). Our victory comes from our faith that Jesus is the son of God. Therefore, when we fix our eyes on Jesus, the great Apostle of our profession, we are guaranteed victory in our daily walk.

Not minding the challenges we face every day of our lives, we are encouraged by the scriptures to persevere so that when we have done the will of God, we will receive what He has promised (Hebrews 10: 36). Keep your faith alive. I want you to know that the One who called us is faithful. He promised never to leave us nor forsake us. He also promised to be with us till the end.

Therefore, if you still have the breath of life in you, hold on tight; that is a sure sign that He is still with you. Remember He promised never to leave you nor forsake you. It doesn't really matter how many people are currently running the race nor how many people that started are still running the race, what matters is that you are still standing for God and His Kingdom and God is standing with you. Success in the race to the kingdom of God is never measured by how many people are faithfully running the race but by how faithful those running the race are. Make sure you stay on track. Remember the words of our Lord Jesus Christ Himself when he said, *"Enter through the narrow gate. For wide is the gate and broad is the road that leads to destruction, and many enter through it. But small is the gate and narrow the road that leads to life, and only a few find it*—Matthew 7:13-14.

POST CHECKPOINT

All Scripture is God-breathed and is useful for teaching, rebuking, correcting and training in righteousness—2 Timothy 2:16. The very next verse after this reads very much like an answer to an implied question. If I am allowed to construct a question that would demand that answer, it would be "why do you say so?"

We know that all scripture is inspired by God and yes we can clearly see what it is intended to be used for, but the question still remains, 'what do we need the teaching and rebuking and correcting and training for?' Why are they 'so' important?

Here is the answer "*so that the servant of God may be thoroughly equipped for every good work*"—2 Timothy 3:17. We understand from the scriptures that "*. . . we are God's handiwork, created in Christ Jesus to do good works, which God prepared in advance for us to do*"—Ephesians 2:10

This can only mean one thing then; the essence of the entire scripture is to prepare us to do those 'good works' which we have been fashioned to do from the beginning of time.

Here is a thought, when next you read any portion of the scripture, ask yourself the four basic questions below and give yourself an honest answer. As you do, you will not only be a benefit to yourself but to others as well (1 Timothy 4:16).

Every scripture you will ever find must fall into one or more of these four basic checkpoints. So, here are the questions we propose and we strongly encourage you to give yourself an honest answer. Whenever I read any part of the scriptures or whenever another believer is talking to me about myself:

- Is there any doctrine I am being taught? Either entirely new or being refreshed
- Is there any sin in my life that I am being rebuked of or any blind spot to be aware of?
- Is there any correction I am supposed to make in my life?
- Is there any training 'exercise' for me to take? Either for myself or to train others.

The beauty of this exercise is that there is always going to be at least a 'yes' answer to one of the above four questions. Our responsibility then is to act in accordance with the word of God concerning the particular checkpoint(s). When we do this and diligently observe the principles promoted by the scriptures (James 1:22) we are guaranteed the result of 2 Timothy 3:17—*Thoroughly equipped for every* (not just some but every) *good work.*

These then are the uses of the entire scriptures. There is no reason again to wonder why the Holy Spirit expressly said through the writings of the Apostle Paul that ". . . *everything that was written in the past was written to teach us, so that through the endurance taught in the Scriptures and the encouragement they provide we might have hope"* Romans 15:4. If we follow the same examples of faith, we'll obtain the same result they did.

Doesn't nature itself tell us that when we read books by doctors and follow exactly what they instructed, we'll end up being doctors?

Same thing happens when we read books by engineers and do exactly what they instructed; we'll end up as engineers.

The best neurosurgeons of this world with the best eye-hand coordination are so because they followed the examples set by their predecessors and did exactly as they were instructed. They cut as outlined and instructed. Sometimes they have to avoid some operations that could endanger certain veins or major arteries and we call them 'the best surgeons in town'. And we could say the same thing for mechanics and accountants or any other profession for that matter.

That same principle applies here—When we follow the examples of the Holy men of God and do exactly as they did, we are guaranteed to obtain the same results (Hebrews 11).